LOVE IS A MEADOW

POEMS

JANE TRASK ROSEN

River Lot Press
Los Angeles, California

ISBN: 979-8-218-61342-6

Cover: Pierre-Auguste Renoir. Meadow (La Prairie), c. 1880. The Barnes
Foundation, BF221

CONTENTS

A Note on the Text

THIS VOLUME contains poems written Jane Trask Rosen between 2006 and 2024. Most of them began during her early-morning walks in the rooftop garden of St. Paul's Towers in Oakland, California.

In addition to those collected here, Jane wrote and often recited poems to commemorate and celebrate friends, family, and others. It is a testament to her productivity that, for reasons of space, only a few of those are excerpted here, in slightly different form.

This edition is dedicated to my mother, whose life, love of words, and enduring creativity (which includes her many sculptures) will be lifelong models for me, my brothers Matthew and Andrew, and her grandchildren David, Gabi, Sam, and Lexi.

Jonathan Freund
Los Angeles
March 2025

In Winter when the ground is white,
The big tall tree is empty quite,
Except for the snowflakes at their play,
Who stay there happily all the day.
The tree then gives a mournful sigh,
He's watching the little snowflakes fly.
He's wishing he had just one little wing,
But he couldn't fly, he's such a big thing.

JANE TRASK
2ND GRADE

Walking on the Roof before Breakfast

You start out your rounds in the darkness.
  Your companions are stars and the moon.
City lights sparkle below you.
  It's chilly and silent. Then, soon,
A tincture of lightness suffuses
  The sky. Stars are dimming. And then
The miracle quietly happens,
  As night turns to day once again.

Triolet: Watering on the Roof

The hose pours out a waterfall:
Our garden in the sky is blessed.
My feet are wet, shoes, socks, and all,
As hose pours out its waterfall.
But flowers smile, trees stand tall,
By sunlight warmed, by winds caressed,
And I provide the waterfall.
Our garden in the sky is blessed.

To a New Plant on the Terrace

I talk to you, water you, feed you.
  I hover and watch you each day.
I tend you whenever you're droopy.
  I worry if I am away.
I don't want your neighbors to crowd you,
  Your life is your own: you need room.
And, as with those other dear children,
  My heart fills with joy as you bloom.

Triolet: To a Building on the San Francisco Skyline, Seen from the Roof

You glimmer as if you were gold,
Across our silent bay.
The dawn may be somber and cold,
But you glimmer as if you were gold.
And the opening day can unfold
In sullen and shadowy grey,
But you glimmer as if you were gold,
By our silent and somnolent bay.

Sonnet to a Hummingbird Encountered on the Roof

You're here! At first you're just a sudden blur
Of motion, unexpected, then I see
Your tiny beak and body, wings awhir:
You've come to share my morning space with me.
But what a journey! Higher than the trees
You had to go, you flew through spinning space,
You braved new skies, explored new galaxies
To join me here upon this rooftop place.
And then I see you leave the roof to rise
Still higher yet, up, up into the sky.
I watch until I lose you in the blue.
You're tiny but you're bolder far than I.
Dear fellow traveler, I realize
It's I who humbly share the world with you.

Triolet: Walking in the Rain

The sky wraps us round in a cloak of grey.
I'm safe in a shadowy world with you.
Is it early or late? Is it night or day?
The sky wraps us round in its cloak of grey,
Reflections glimmer along the way,
And falling drops beat a soft tattoo.
The sky wraps us round in a cloak of grey.
I'm safe in this shadowy world with you.

Grandchildren

We treasure smiles, tears,
hugs, but learn late your true gift
to us: the future.

Afterwards

Is it just ozone?
Or is the air's quick, bright smell
the storm's sweet blessing?

Evening on the Roof

Pale and still, the sky
is a shy maiden, caressed
by the setting sun.

Mt. Tamalpais

The mountain's round top
breaks through fog, like a whale's back
cresting the grey sea.

San Francisco's Skyline

Fogged in, hazed over,
your pale geometry is
still mysterious.

Foggy Mornings

Oakland's hills pull down
warm grey caps over their eyes
to keep themselves warm.

To the Sequoias

Sunshine, water, fire,
fed you, silent giants. Now
you nourish our souls.

October

Rain feeds parched meadows,
softly hides cities' noises,
comforts us, soothes us.

It's Come at Last

It's come at last! It's really here!
You're in your double-digit year.
Ten is magic now and then:
Heroines in books are ten,
Ten's a cinch to multiply,
Ten tops the charts and hits the sky.
You're growing up, in heart and mind.
Early childhood's left behind,
Teen-hood looms ahead of you.
But while you're ten, there's lots to do:
You can laugh and cry and sing and play
And read and dance the days away.
You're not too young and you're not too old.
Your games can be silly, your dreams can be bold.
So just keep being *you*, from dawn until night.
And I wish you a year full of love and delight.

To a Sister Turning 75

Early morning walks,
attic rooms, dog show,
milkweed pillows, made-up games,
hidden sandpile, borrowed books,
white horse. What would I
have done without you?

Years

As birthdays come and go, I stay the same.
My teen-aged longings, challenges, and fears
Are with me still, my childhood needs remain.
A hug still comforts, and a smile cheers.
The heart's delights have neither thinned nor greyed,
My joys are not less sunny, nor my tears
Less salty. And the mystery still remains:
The slow and silent passage of the years.

What Is Love?

Love is a buttercup
Under the chin,
Love is a meadow,
A stream,

Love is a giggle,
A wink and a nod,
Love is a secret,
A dream,

Love is a circus,
A merry-go-round,
Love is a birthday
Balloon,

Love is an aria,
Love is a song,
A melody's echo,
A tune,

Love is a flower
That blooms in the snow,
Love is a torch in
The dark,

Love is a vessel
When waters are deep,
Love is a refuge,
An ark,

Love is a mystery,
Conquering time,
Outlasting the years and
The days.

If you have been loved
And have loved in return,
Love stays in your heart
Always

To the Hummingbird, Encountered Again on the Roof

The wind has blown the clouds away
And blown the stars from the sky,
Leaves are awhirl, treetops advance.
You are here again, up high,
So tiny, so bold, so unafraid,
At home in the wild sky.

To the Silliest Plant on the Roof

Ridiculous cabbage! Your cones poke up in the air
      Like a lavender jester's cap, and all the while
You brandish a spiky stalk with a yellow flair:
      Dear silliest flower, thank you for making me smile!

To the Full Moon, Seen from the Roof

Your face seems strangely quizzical,
Silent and cold and free,
But question and answer are lost in space,
A brilliant mystery.

Ode to a Virus

Was it really so awful, really so bad?
        We were given three meals every day!
And just think of the wonderful things we could do
        To while the long hours away:

We could write all our relatives, call up our friends,
        We could lie around sleeping till noon,
We could clean off our desks, and read all those books
        We've been saving to read "sometime soon,"

We could follow the exercise tapes twice a day,
        With moves and positions gymnastic,
We could set out our elegant China and glass
        To bring cheer as we ate off of plastic,

We could sweep up our terraces, talk to our plants,
        We could balance our checkbooks with care,
We could start on our taxes, or dust all our shelves,
        Or hand wash our best underwear,

We could clean out our closets for clothes to discard,
        Like that silly old, frilly old bonnet,
We could practice a dance, we could make up a song,
        We could write a haiku or a sonnet,

We could thank St. Paul's Towers for caring for us,
        And its staff for their efforts and cheer.
We all did our best, we all passed the test,
        And we'll all have a Happy New Year!

Elegy

The world is emptier without you here,
Beloved friend. We miss your lovely face,
We miss your dancing eyes, your buoyant cheer:
The world is emptier without you here.
You showed us courage in the face of fear,
You gave us energy, compassion, grace.
The world is emptier without you here,
Beloved friend. We miss your lovely face.

Arrowhead

Ancient roots are sentinels by day,
Starry skies keep watch on us by night.
There's food and laughter, poems, and games to play,
As ancient roots are sentinels by day.
The pasts we share become a bright array,
Our hearts unfold, and memory holds us tight;
Ancient roots are sentinels by day
And starry skies keep watch on us by night.

Lake Merritt, Seen from Above

Elegant at night,
she wears her shining pearls
in a double chain of lights,
one tranquil and still, one
below, shimmering.

Watersong

What would it be like without April's sweet rain?
  Or December's soft flakes that come falling again?
  Or the dew on the grass? Or the mist on the sea?

No lemonade stands, no billowing grain,
  No bubble baths, mud pies, or hot cups of tea,
  No clean streets or clean laundry, and never again

To build sandcastles, run at the edge of the sea
  Where the waves chase our toes. We would ache with the pain
  Of lost splashes and dives, we would wonder in vain

Where yesterday's tidepools have gone. You and me
  Know our lifeblood is water, a blessing to see
  And to treasure. Be thankful for April's soft rain.

Triolet: The Moment Between

Chilly and silent, the moon in the sky
Keeps watch on our slumbering city below.
Is it day? Is it night? It is neither. Up high,
Chilly and silent, the moon in the sky
Is fading, the stars have all gone, by and by,
In the east there's a tender, diaphanous glow.
Chilly and silent, the moon in the sky
Keeps watch on our wakening city below.

Pantoum: Before Morning

The fog on the hills sits heavy and grey,
A blanket of darkness still hangs in the sky.
Will the sun ever rise? Will it ever be day?
The clock says it ought to be morning, so why
Does a blanket of darkness still hang in the sky?
I'm waiting and wondering, dangling in space;
The clock says it ought to be morning, so why
Is the sun so unwilling to show us his face?
I'm waiting and wondering, caught in the space
Between darkness and daylight, mysterious, still,
And the sun is unwilling to show us his face.
The air should be warming, not somber and chill,
Between darkness and daylight, mysterious, still.
Will the sun ever rise? Will it ever be day?
The air should be warming, not somber and chill,
But the fog on the hills is still heavy and grey.

Epithalamium

There may be a world that is certain,
But it's not the dear world we have here:
Though tonight is a special bright moment in time,
Days ahead may be cloudy or clear.

Suns rise and suns set, and each morning
May bring us a smile or a tear,
But we have what we have, and our most precious gift
Is to love what we have, without fear,

For the wheel will keep turning and turning,
Each hour and each day and each year.
So you two who will marry, your love is a blessing
That shines on us all, far and near.

Early Morning Fog

No stars, no moon,
No city lights below,
No buildings, bridges, nothing eye can see,
Only a cloak of grey
Whose soft embrace
Enfolds us in its silent mystery.

To a Plant Moved to the Roof

Poor little yellow rosebush,
You pined away in shade.
You couldn't blossom, you could only
Fade.
My little pale companion,
I've moved you to a place
Where you'll have light and air to breath
And space.
Dear little yellow rosebush,
Now that you have room,
Now that you have sunshine,
Bloom.

Santa Fe Memories

Fiery sunsets.
Monarchs of baked red earth. Clouds.
Poetry. Laughter.

Gold Rush

Gold nuggets, gold hills,
Old towns, new wines, giant trees,
Goddesses: friendship.

Midnight

Oakland is sleeping,
Hills snuggled in downy mist,
Nightlights low. Sweet dreams!

To a Younger Sister

A golden plaything
To care for and love, became
My sister, my friend.

Summer House Closet

Stiff slickers, high boots,
Fishing poles, canes, hats, old maps,
Echoes of days, years.

Memo from a Trip

The world is so full of new places
To encounter when I go away:
New scenery, foods, and new faces.
The world is so full of new places,
New vistas, new habits, new graces,
New attitudes. Yet I can say
Though the world is abrim with new places,
I miss you when I am away.

One Nation, Indivisible: A Meditation on Proposition 8

It seems we are divisible after all.
We are two separate nations,
    one with the freedom to be who we are,
    one without that freedom.
But we are not done with the fight.
The battle is not over,
The banner still waves proudly above our heads.
If you think we will stop, think again:
The world has already changed,
    and will continue to change.
We have joined the ranks of brave men and women
    who have fought and died for their rights over the years.
Freedom is seldom a gift.
It is more often a hard-won prize after a long and bloody battle.
But why should it be such a struggle?
What we want is not really so much:
What we want is only liberty and justice for all.

Dear Friend

Your struggles are over, dear friend,
But the world seems an emptier place
Without you. And now, at the end,
Though your struggles are over, dear friend,
I miss you. I miss the rare blend
Of calm and delight in your face.
Your struggles are over, dear friend,
But the world is an emptier place.

In Praise of Winter . . . and Love

Hands are scrunched down into pockets,
And hats are pulled down over ears,
Our teeth are a-chatter, our noses a-drip,
And our eyes are a-brimming with tears,
The stars are bright icicles set in
The frozen expanse of the sky.
But our hearts are still beating, our spirits still warm:
We have life, we have love, you and I.

Song of Lost Objects

The glasses I searched for so diligently
      Are discovered, secure on my head.
The book I was reading last evening till midnight
      Waits patiently under the bed.

The puppy that wandered too far from the picnic
      Comes wagging back, safe and alive.
The twin that was drowned in Illyria's shipwreck
      Strolls back on the stage, in Act V.

The ring that slid off in the garden last autumn
      Lies quietly under the snow,
To surface again in the spring. So I wonder . . .
      Just where did my childhood go?

Where are the songs we sang round the piano?
      Where are the clothes on the line?
Where are the hugs and the giggles, the dreaming,
      The splashes, the hands that held mine?

Where is the comfort of newly baked cookies,
      The thrill of the bright birthday bow?
If the lost will be found and the longed-for returned,
      Oh, where did my childhood go?

Why Walking on the Roof is Never Boring

Each minute brings a change of light,
Each circle round moves Time along.
The world keeps changing, dark or bright.
Each minute brings a change of light.
The air's alive, the moment's right,
Moon, clouds, and hills all sing their song.
Each minute brings a change of light,
Each circle round moves Time along.

To Plants on the Roof after a Windy Night

I was safe in my bed last night,
    While you were wild and free,
Tumbling and whirling and rolling around,
    With the stars for company.
You danced out the soles of your shoes last night,
    While the moon looked on to see.
And now you are quiet, resting at last
    From your night of revelry.

La Ronde

Sleeping and waking
We measure the years,
Laughing and crying
In smiles and tears.
Searching and finding
Through pleasure and pain,
Planting and reaping
In sunshine and rain.
Forgetting, remembering
Promises, things,
Wondering, wandering,
Winters and springs.
Coming and going
As day follows day,
Loving and caring
As long as we may.

On Seeing Squirrels Cavorting in the Trees Outside the Dining Room

Jumping, chattering,
Tumbling around,
Squealing, quarreling,
Falling to the ground:

Why do they fascinate
And charm us so?
Do we recognize the children
We were long ago?

Plea to Venus

Dear planet, you are hung above the hills,
A brilliant beacon in the silent night.
The stars are dimming. Dawn is on its way.
But you, our guardian, are blazing bright.
You are the star of love. Watch over us
Till darkness fades into the morning light.

To Birds Singing Before Dawn

What tells you that the time is right?
It's dark and chilly and feels like night,
Above the stars are still shining bright,
But you are awake below,
Singing your hearts out, brave and clear,
To herald the dawn that has yet to appear,
Loudly enough for all to hear.
You sing, so it must be so.
We only know what our clocks can say.
So how do you know it will soon be day,
That the stars will dim and then fade away,
A secret we'll never know?

On Making a Clay Relief of a Stone Carving

You were carved in stone
Nine centuries ago,
High on a cathedral wall,
Caressed by wind and rain.
Your head is bent in study,
Your hands are huge and still,
So rugged and so elegant,
So intricate and plain.
I work with you in silence,
I live with you in love,
Together we will conquer time
And you will live again.

Thanksgiving

We're stiffer, we're forgetting,
Sleeping less and aching more,
So do we sometimes wonder
What it is we're grateful for?
Here is the answer: memories
Of love that never ends,
For grandparents and cousins,
For parents, siblings, friends,
For games we played and plans we made
And silly songs we sung,
For puppies that we tumbled with,
Vacations, summer fun,
For wrapping birthday presents,
For love that came to stay . . .
Once in our hearts, still in our lives,
Yesterday, today.

Song of the Books

We wait for you quietly,
Hoping you'll come.
Serene on our shelves
We are patient and dumb,
But open us up,
Explore us, you'll find
Delights for your heart
And rewards for your mind:
Murderers, lovers,
Myths of the ages
Are waiting for you
In our beautiful pages,
Histories, mysteries,
Large print and small,
Poems, romances,
Biographies . . . all.
So borrow us, read us,
Enjoy us, and then,
Return us so others
Can love us again!

How Do We Stay Alive?

Mondays come and Mondays go
      And Tuesdays close behind,
Then Wednesdays, Thursdays, Fridays
      Follow after in a blind
Procession. So what keeps us from
      Becoming dull, with eye
And ear and heart becoming dead,
      As Time meanders by?
It's you, my son, and you, my daughter,
      You, my friends, my dears,
Who keep us whole, who bless our days
      As they turn into years;
It's love that keeps the hours
      Moving onward, come what may,
And keeps us breathing in and out,
      Forever and a day.

Triolet on Birthdays

We say a birthday's just another day.
But is the child still alive within
Who loves balloons and singing, loves to play?
We say a birthday's just another day,
We're casual and calm, we brush away
Congratulations, as the cards come in.
We say a birthday's just another day,
But is a child still alive within?

Hodgepodge

Tables and chairs,
Dishes and spoons,
Midnights and mornings,
Evenings and noons,
Mountains and meadows,
Forests and streams,
Fantasies, fallacies,
Blessings and dreams.

Dear Poetry

Dear poetry, dear poetry,
     You hold our hearts in thrall,
You're silly and your solemn,
     You're a wonder to us all.

You cheer us and you challenge us,
     You bless us with delight,
You soothe us and you comfort us,
     You see us through the night.

You open hidden doors to us,
     You recognize our fears,
Our griefs, our loves, our loneliness,
     Our laughter, and our tears.

You sang to us as children,
     You'll stay with us to the end,
Our teacher and our counsellor,
     Our lover and our friend.

Counting-Out Rhyme (I)

Higgledy Piggledy Pie,
The moon is up in the sky,
Your face is red,
It's time for bed,
Higgledy Piggledy Pie.

Hickory Dickory Dare,
The pudding's up in the air,
Put on your gown
And go to town,
Hickory Dickory Dare.

Hey Diddle Diddle Delight,
The pig flew off in the night,
Jack and Jill
Have paid the bill,
Hey Diddle Diddle Delight.

Hobbledy Bobbledy Boo,
The cow is tying her shoe,
My mousie gray
Has run away,
Hobbledy Bobbledy Boo.

Lippity Loppity Loy,
A girl's as good as a boy,
Now one, two, three,
It's time for tea,
Lippity Loppity Loy.

Companions in the Sky

It's early and it's cool. The city sleeps
       In darkness yet, but I am not alone:
Capella, Rigel, Sirius are here
       Above me, and the Queen is on her throne,

Orion, mighty Hunter, strides the sky,
       His Dog beside him, and the giant Bear
Patrols the heavens, circling round the Pole,
       His footprints brilliant in the starry air,

The Pleiades, dear faithful sisters all,
       Are clustered in the night, and there above
The Lion watches with the Twins beside.
       I walk beneath them. They look down with love.

Take Your Time

Time is a mystery.
It bends and stiffens,
      expands and contracts
      to a rhythm that has nothing to do
      with the beat of the metronome.
We cannot measure time by the clock.

For instance:
      20 minutes is a long time to
            hold one's breath,
            wait in a doctor's office or a supermarket line,
            walk in shoes that pinch,
            stand in the rain with no coat,
            listen to a boring lecture.
      But it is a short time to
            cuddle a newborn grandchild,
            read a good book,
            explore Paris or Rome,
            enjoy a Thanksgiving dinner with your family,
            mourn a loved one who has died.

So don't mess with time,
      let it flow as it will and move at its own speed.
It is precious to us all.

Love Letter to 2011

We've waited so long for you! Now that you're here,
With new days and new weeks and new months (a whole year!),
We welcome the gifts that the calendar brings,
And we thank you for all of these wonderful things:
A cup of hot cocoa on wintery days,
Good books and good movies, some operas, some plays,
A smile from our children, a hug from our grands,
A nod from a friend and a clasping of hands,
A cozy, soft blanket to cover our bed,
A welcoming pillow to cushion our head,
No falls and no quarrels, hurt feelings or tears,
No sleeplessness, tummy aches, worries or fears,
No lost keys or lost glasses, no moments of sadness.
But heads full of memories, hearts full of gladness,
Grateful for health and happy we're here,
Ready to ring in another new year!

Moving Along (I)

Crayons and paint boxes,
    Counting out rhymes,
Poems and riddles,
    Pennies and dimes.

Doll houses, Valentines,
    Teddy bears, clay,
Tricycles, bicycles,
    Peddling away.

Puppies and guinea pigs,
    Turtles and mice,
Hopscotch and roller skates,
    Marbles and dice.

Adding, subtracting,
    Skills to be learned,
Schoolwork and homework
    And grades to be earned.

Waking and sleeping
    By night and by day,
Falling in love
    One astonishing day.

Mornings and evenings,
    Winters and springs,
Giving, receiving
    Wonderful things.

Forgiving, forgetting
    A tune and a song,
Childhood, adulthood,
    Years move along.

Memory like a River

Memory, like a moving river,
Winds on through our life's long dream;
Some bits of our past are lost forever,
Lodged somewhere too far upstream.
But sometimes, unasked, our rolling river
Upheaves as it flows along,
A gift we believed was lost forever . . .
A name, a moment, a song.

In Praise of Wrinkles

If life is an aria, sung from the heart,
The lines in our faces belong
To the music. Those webbings and creases are part
Of the sweet composition that wanders along
As we live, they are part of the symphony's art,
Adding richness and depth to the song.

Hymn to Laundry

Washing and wringing and scrubbing away,
Seems to go on for ever and ever.
We're linked to our mothers' and grandmothers' day
By washing and wringing and scrubbing away.
But we're part of a past even further away,
We're sisters to women who knelt by a river,
Washing and wringing and scrubbing away.
It's a ritual that has enthralled us forever.

Gardenful of Treats

Asparagus and artichokes,
      Radishes, tomatoes,
Cauliflower, carrots, corn,
      Pumpkins and potatoes,
Sweet peas and chickpeas,
      Lentils and zucchini,
Beans of course (green and lima,
      Kidney, cannellini),
Eggplant, okra, turnips,
      Leeks so white and pale,
Celery and spinach,
      Cabbage, peppers, kale,
Parsnips and rose hips,
      Onions, mushrooms, beets,
Rutabaga, broccoli:
      A gardenful of treats!

Whirlwind

Tops spin,
dreidels,
  tumbleweeds too,

bike wheels,
  maypoles,
  yellow and blue,

dervishes,
  merry-go-rounds,
  whirlpools blue,

our earth . . .
  and maybe
  the stars spin too.

Hold onto Memories

Do you remember jumping rope,
    Hopscotch and trading cards?
Roller skates and Kick-the-Can
    Played out through neighbors' yards?
Picnics and singing silly songs,
    Crayons, scissors, glue?
When these dear memories are gone,
    Will we be lost then too?

Even Flowers Have their Battles to Fight

You're struggling along, little rosebush,
And I'm here to help, as you strive
To regain all your strength and your beauty
From the pests that would eat you alive.
I want you to win, little rosebush,
Be green and start blooming, survive.
Be healthy, be strong, be a fighter.
Recover.
        Shout "Victory!"
            Thrive.

Singing the Blues

Blackberries picked from their bushes
        Are juicy and tender and sweet,
Raspberries mixed with sugar and cream
        Are always a pleasure to eat,
Strawberry jam is tasty,
        And strawberry shortcake's a treat.
But blueberries bring us the color
        Of lapis and oceans and skies,
They're always nutritious, delicious
        In muffins and pancakes and pies,
They deliver a boost to our memory,
        They donate new sight to our eyes.
So blueberries win the blue ribbon,
        And blueberries take First Prize!

Sunday Night Cookie Torment

You lie in wait for us every week.
We try not to listen, but still you speak.
Have you no modesty? Have you no shame?
Why do you silently call my name?
You sit on your plate, so serene, so quiet.
Does cookie-speak have no word for *diet*?

Early Morning Mist

Not quite a drizzle,
Not yet a rain,
Just a gentle caress
That now and again
Bestows on our cheeks
And our foreheads as well
Its soft benediction
That says, "All is well,
You're alive, you are loved,
You are beautiful, free."
It's the morning's sweet blessing
For you and for me.

To the Clay Room

What magic energy fills this room,
And flows around us all,
Inhabits the clay and animates
Our pieces, large and small?
What moves our hands, infuses our tools,
Enfolds our hearts, so we
Can look and listen and labor to find
What we can bring to be?
What breathes at last through finished work
That rests on counters and shelves?
It's the spirit of effort . . . and learning . . . and love . . .
And the courage to find ourselves.

Admonition

Scan the sky,
See what comes,
Sunshine or fog or rain.

Hustle and bustle,
Hurry and scurry,
Through wonder and pleasure and pain.

You can like it or lump it,
Embrace it or shove it,
Debate or berate or complain,

But only remember:
Whatever the weather,
This day will not be here again.

The Playground

Things go wrong,
      And then things go right:
It rains all day
      And then clears at night,
You lose your glasses
      Somewhere on Sunday,
Then buy a new pair
      That's better on Monday,
Your best friend seems
      In a cranky mood,
Then dinner at night's
      Your favorite food,
Your daughter's too busy
      To take your call,
But her loving letter
      Makes up for it all.

When we were young
      We loved the swings,
But the seesaw prepared us
      For what life brings.

Syllable Syllabub
Best read aloud

unreal, unravel, unrest,
beneath, befuddle, bequest,

abandon, abrasion, abash,
penumbra, penuche, panache,

corruption, correction, caress,
fandango, fantasia, finesse,

resemble, resistance, result,
occlusion, occasion, occult,

marauder, marimba, maroon,
belabor, ballistic, balloon,

inclement, inclosure, incline,
confusing, configure, confine,

salacious, salami, salute,
galoshes, galumphing, galoot,

atrocious, attrition, attempt,
uncover, uncommon, unkempt,

resourceful, recycle, recite,
delicious, delinquent, delight,

abounding, abysmal, absurd --
oh, wonderful, warbling word!

A Lesson in Opposites

Up & down,
 In & out,
Sleeping, waking,
 Whisper, shout,
Closed & open,
 Square & round,
Reward & punish,
 Lost & found,
Working, playing,
 Sunshine, rain,
Winter, summer,
 Pleasure, pain,
Starting, stopping,
 Hopes & fears,
Knowledge, wonder,
 Laughter, tears,
Compliant, stubborn,
 Ease & stress,
But mostly love . . .
 Or loneliness.

Pairs (I)

Up and down, in and out,
waking, sleeping, whisper, shout,
old and new, night and day,
cold and hot, work and play,

noon and midnight, wet and dry,
spending, saving, earth and sky,
living, dying, happy, sad,
early, late, despairing, glad,

forget, remember, heavy, light,
starting, ending, courage, fright,
teaching, learning, all the time,
songs that sing and words that rhyme.

It Seems Freud was Right

Love and work -- we need them both
(Freud tells us again and again).
They both can be challenging, easy or hard,
They both can bring pleasure or pain.
But without them we're colder and darker,
We're wandering lost in the rain.

Night's Blessing

Sun sets, moon rises,
       Clouds float by,
Stars dance their nightly waltz,
       Around the sky.
Rain falls, snow falls,
       Leaves drift down,
Birds settle, lights dim
       Around the town.
Doors close, children sleep,
       Warm in their beds,
Dreams keep us company
       Inside our heads.

Turning Back the Clock

Would you go back if you could?
A day or a month or a year?
Would you feel again
All that teen-age pain,
Or your childhood's gasping fear?
Maybe we ought to forego
Our search for a vanishing star,
And decide to stay
Right here in today
And to be the age that we are.

My Beautiful Boys
A clay relief in progress

As I struggle to recover
I stand on the edge of a cliff,
        fearful of being tumbled off into the dizzying void,
        lost in whirling space,
        spinning out of control.

You two bring me back
        to a world of safety.
You rescue me.
You anchor me.

You two, here with the others,
        the coy fox warbling her aria,
        the smooth burnished body of wordless grief,
        the loving gesture, child reaching up, mother leaning to embrace,
        the two strong and simple columned figures,
        the woman with her blooming forest of hair,

You two, my beautiful boys,
        with your tilted heads,
        your hands, reaching and gesturing,
        and your elbows and knees akimbo,
        resting every which way on the rocks,

You are anchored in your space
And so you anchor me in mine.

You bring me back from the cliff edge

And the void of uncertainty.
You bring me back to the solid world
    of gravity and trusted ground,
Where the cliff is there,
    not to betray us,
But to provide a path upwards,
    through imagination and courage,
    to certainty.

You beckon and I follow.
We are family, you and I,
    because, of course, once, long ago,
    we were all clay.

You rescue me, my beautiful boys.

My beautiful boys.

A New Pair

Dear sneakers, you're lovely,
        You cushion my feet,
Put a spring in my step
        As I'm crossing the street,
Your canvas is shiny,
        Your laces are clean,
You're the brightest, the whitest
        New shoes to be seen!

To my old pair: you lasted
        A year, stood the test,
You gave me good service --
        Now have a good rest!

Too Many to Count

How many days did I have you?
How many weeks and years?
How many cups of coffee?
How many smiles and tears?
How many rainy evenings?
How many sunny days?
They're countless. And now I miss you
In numberless, countless ways.

Replacement Parts
(internal organs and internal rhymes)

In earlier days we were always amazed
At what surgeons were able to do.
It was really fantastic that metal or plastic
Could make an old body part new.
But now no one laughs at implants or grafts,
A new shoulder is taken in stride.
New noses and lips, new knees and new hips --
Nothing we want is denied.
Now quick as a wink we're all in the pink,
With new bits that the doctor delivers,
We can make a new start with a freshly made heart
And we'll soon have new lungs and new livers!
You may hear some chuckles for gorgeous new knuckles,
Which soon will be taken for granted.
But what can we do to make our brains new?
Could a memory chip be implanted?

Lullaby

Slippers, slappers,
clippers, clappers,
jumping, bumping,
limping, lumping,
singing, ringing,
sinking, thinking,
knitters, twitters,
hooters, hitters,
strumming, drumming,
cramming, coming,
dashing, crashing,
spilling, splashing,
footers, headers,
off to bedders!

Merry-Go-Round

Sing a song of springtime,
Playing in the sun,
Butterflies and roller skates,
School is almost done.
Sing a song of summer,
Barefoot girls and boys
Building roads and castles
With favorite sandbox toys.
Sing a song of autumn,
Greens becoming brown,
Turkey's in the oven,
Leaves are falling down.
Sing a song of winter,
Icicles and snow,
New Year's resolutions,
As round and round we go.
Sing a song of days and nights,
Weave a magic spell,
Months revolve and seasons turn:
Nature's carousel.

Dear Friend, Don't Go

Dear friend, don't go. Please stay a while!
        I need you here with me.
Without you winds blow colder,
        And hours drag endlessly,
And dawns are dark and noons are dull,
        And eyes are bright with tears.
Your cheerfulness embraces me,
        You smile belies your years.
We walk together, talk together,
        As time keeps ticking by.
And when your time has come, it will be
        You who know, not I.
And if your time is near, my wish
        For you: a peaceful end.
I'll have you always in my heart,
        A part of me, dear friend.

Timeline

It may be threescore years and ten:
        That's what they used to say.
But numbers cannot calculate
        How long we have to stay.
It may be years, it may be months,
        It may be only days,
So don't depend on tomorrows
        Or count up yesterdays.

It's the moment that's precious, the now that is dear:
    If we listen, our heartbeats will say,
Do what you love and love what you do,
    For we only have today.

Good Friends

Little Miss Muffet and Little Bo Peep
And Little Boy Blue, who fell asleep,

Jack and Jill, and Tigger and Pooh,
Dorothy and Toto, Mowgli, Baloo,

Robin Hood and his merry men,
Living the life in Sherwood's glen,

Mary Poppins, and Ratty and Mole,
Alice and friends in the rabbit's hole . . .

You were my friends in years gone by.
We had some adventures, you and I.

Where are you now? Are you old and ill?
Or are you beguiling and youthful still?
Do hands still hold you, hearts still beat
To your challenges, triumphs, your loves so sweet?

I loved you then. Could it be true,
For a moment in time, you loved me too?

Wanderlust

Trains and planes and motor bikes,
Ships that sail the seas,
Tricycles and bicycles,
And roller skates and skis,

Trucks and buses, trolley cars,
Kayaks and canoes,
Hot air balloons and inner tubes,
Boots and ballet shoes,

A pogo stick, a camel,
A donkey or a horse,
Sleds and sleighs and sliding trays,
Our own two feet (of course),

Chinese junks and balsa rafts,
Rides at a county fair . . .
All are magic carpets
To take us anywhere!

Gratitude

For sunsets and sunrises year after year,
For days that are sunny and skies that are clear,

For a comfortable chair and comfortable shoes,
For Mozart sonatas and Monet's soft blues,

For a cup of hot tea on a blustery day,
A night of good sleep to whisk worries away,

For puppies we played with and soft little kittens,
Warm socks and warm sweaters and warm wooly mittens,

For babies who hugged us and teachers who cared,
For parents and siblings and games that we shared,

For children who grew up in fits and in starts,
And surely for friends . . . who reside in our hearts.

In Times of Drought

A drip, a drop,
        a torrent,
Cascades,
        a waterfall,
A rainy day,
        a drizzle,
A hurricane,
        a squall,
Water is life
        for man and beast,
And life is love for all.

Song of the Years

Giving, taking,
Back and forth,
Sleeping, waking,
South and north,

Smiling, frowning,
Foolish, wise,
Cloudy mornings,
Sunny skies,

Ups and downs,
Ins and outs,
Laughter, tears,
Whispers, shouts,

Coming, going,
Dark and light,
Losing, finding,
Day and night,

Sad and happy,
Work and play.
Today, tomorrow,
Yesterday.

Couples: A Valentine

Adam & Eve and Jack & Jill,
The Tortoise & the Hare,
Gilbert & Sullivan, Dick & Jane –
Couples are everywhere!

There's Romeo & Juliet,
Holmes & Watson too,
The Prince & the Pauper, Lewis & Clark –
Everything's two-by-two!

Hansel & Gretel, Currier & Ives,
Scarlett O'Hara & Rhett,
The Owl & the Pussycat, Bonnie & Clyde –
And we're not finished yet!

Batman & Robin, Rogers & Hart,
Robin Hood & Little John,
Tippecanoe & Tyler too –
The list goes on and on!

Two by two, we boarded the Ark:
Was that when it all began –
The power of two for me and you,
For every woman and man!

Moving Along (II)

Skipping and jumping and running,
    Tossing and kicking a ball,
Cutting and pasting and drawing,
    And reading and writing and all,

Slipping and sliding and hopping,
    Losing and finding again,
Waking and sleeping and dreaming,
    Singing in sunshine and rain,

Wondering, wishing, and wanting
    In myriad different ways,
Living and loving and laughing,
    Through mornings and evenings and days,

Coming and going and growing,
    In smiles and giggles and tears –
The mystery of child to adult,
    The mystery of days and of years.

Mysteries

Falling snow is a mystery:
It changes a world of brown
Into magical landscapes of blue and white,
Swirling and drifting down.

Foggy mornings and evenings
Are another mystery:
They wrap our world and enfold us all
In silence and secrecy.

Buds on trees are a mystery:
How that tiny hard little thing
Can emerge from a brittle branch one day
And turn the world into spring.

Zero is one of the mysteries:
It changes one to ten,
Or changes ten to a million,
Then changes it back again.

And then there's the mystery of children:
How can sister and brother,
Same genes, same family, as they grow
Be so different from each other?

Love is the greatest mystery:
How can it still be true
That your heart sings that you love me
And mine that I love you?

Sleep On

I am awake in the lovely pre-dawn chill,
But you are still sleeping, warm and dark and still.
I breathe the morning, but you still breathe the night,
My dreams have faded, but yours are with you still.

Sleep on, you sleepers, and may your dreams be bright
With comfort and safety, filled with happy light.
So they should be. But if they are filled with fear
And demons instead, those terrible mares of the night,

Send your dreams flying. Send them all up to me here.
I will exchange them for visions of innocent cheer
And happy adventures. Slumber on. Lie still.
Dream on, you dreamers, dream. The way is clear.
Sleep on, you sleepers, sleep. The day is near.

To an Aphid

You hide under leaves. You kill roses.
You lurk like a thief in the dark.
You offer the gardener nothing.
So who let you onto the ark?

Childhood Games

Where have they gone, those lovely games?
Remember the rules? Remember the names?

> Hopscotch and Marbles,
> Jacks, Old Maid,
> Hide and Seek
> In the sun and shade,
> Slap Jack, Tag,
> And Dodge Ball too,
> Jump Rope rhymes,
> Some old, some new,
> Kick the Can and
> Blind Man's Buff.
> We never tired
> Or had enough.

All those games we used to play,
Summer evenings, day after day,
Sidewalk rituals under the sky:
We lived them and loved them, you and I.

On Finishing a Good Book (I)

Dear book, you have been a companion
    From the first to the very end,
You were always there beside me,
    My sister, my lover, my friend.

And now that I'm ready to leave you,
    I'll put you back on the shelf
With a tinge of sadness, as if I
    Were losing a part of myself.

I've loved being with you. I'll miss you.
    Good luck in whatever you do.
And as you find other new readers,
    Will you miss me a little too?

Itinerary

King of Prussia, Chinchilla,
       Ho-Ho-Kus and Honalee,
Ketchikan, Hoonah, and Skagway,
       Burnt Corn and Bumble Bee,

Southampton, Westport, and Eastham,
       Northridge and Ochlocknee,
Copperopolis, Killybegs, Zagreb,
       Kalamazoo, Truckee,

Anza Borrego and Gobi,
       Sahara and Kara Kum too,
Negev, Ordos, Kalahari,
       Death Valley, Mohave, Karoo,

Pacific, Atlantic, Aegean,
       Indian, Arctic as well . . .
Now where are we going to travel today?
       Wherever we want. Who can tell?

To A China Pig, Rediscovered

Little China piggy,
      With your little China smile,
When I was young you came to me
      And stayed with me a while.

Days were simpler, summers longer,
      Sun and rain and snow,
A safer world for you and me -
      Where did it all go?

Little China piggy,
      With your little China ears,
What happened to the wondering,
      The laughter and the tears?

Sleep was easy, time was free,
      For coming and for going.
Those days are gone, but we are here,
      Remembering and knowing.

Haiku to the Roof Garden

On your peaceful path
my heart sings and words start their
own rounds in my head.

Life Story

Bumping and thumping,
  Singing and swinging,
Skipping and jumping,
  Ending, beginning,

Knowing and going,
  Blinking and winking,
Glittering, glowing,
  Wondering, thinking,

Weeping and sleeping,
  Growing and giving,
Caring, preparing,
  As long as we're living.

So What Was It with Paper Dolls?

What was it? It wasn't the dresses and coats.
        (When we were young, clothes were a bore!)
It wasn't the cutting. Could it be the Tabs?
        Were they magic? Did they keep the score?

Tabs on the shoulders, Tabs on the waist,
        Tabs on the head and each shoe.
Those Tabs had the power to make your doll live —
        Each day she could be someone new.

Be careful! Don't cut off a Tab! If you do,
        Your dolly has nothing to wear.
But crease the Tab carefully, fold it in place,
        There she is! and you've done it with flair.

To a Cup of Tea

You comfort me, quiet me,
       Let me slow down
When I'm moving too fast.
       You can smooth out a frown
For a moment and give me
       A smile instead.
You can calm down the thoughts
       That carouse in my head.
Your heat warms my hands
       And my inner realms too.
Thanks for your friendship.
       I'm grateful to you.

To a Beloved Bear

Dear Teddy, you were my companion.
       How long ago it seems!
You were always there beside me,
       Sharing my bed and my dreams.
You were patient and uncomplaining,
       As I carried you everywhere,
And if you got left behind sometimes
       You always stayed right there.
I cried with you, laughed with you, hugged you.
       You stayed with me faithfully.
When I reach the end of my journey,
       Will I find you waiting for me?

To an African Violet

You're supposed to be difficult, tricky to raise,
    But here on my table you thrive.
You are upright and beautiful, graceful and strong,
    You're in deep purple bloom. You're alive.
Thanks for your confidence. If I'm depressed,
    Or struggling with anger or grief,
I'll feel better to know that you gave me a gift:
    Your trust in me and your belief.

Ode to Matisse's Etruscan Vase

You share the room with so much else! Matisse
Was not just painting you. His brush caressed
The sunshine pouring in, art on the walls,
Lemons and oranges, the lady dressed
For comfort, open book before her laid,
Her cheek on hands, in thoughtful reverie.
What was he painting? Who can know his mind,
Or analyze his brilliant artistry?

Breathing

Breathing in and breathing out,
   For minutes, hours, years,
Through springs and winters, days and nights,
   Through laughter and through tears,

Breathing in and breathing out,
   Through sunshine and through rain,
Through sleeping, waking, youth and age,
   Through pleasure and through pain,

Breathing in and breathing out,
   Through shadow and through sun,
And then between the in and out . . . .
   It stops.
         And we are done.

Walking After the Rain

Puddles below us and puddles above us,
      Dampness infusing the air,
Driplets and droplets of moisture,
      Sogginess everywhere.
Water is life and life is love.
      The storm is over and done,
Leaving its dew to caress us
      And bless us, everyone.

Lentando

We were fast when we were young,
We ran through days and years,
We skipped through every happiness,
We tore through pain and tears.

But now that we are slowing down,
We're finding more and more
Those moments free of speed and stress
And times of peace and quietness
We never knew before.

On Slowing Down

I've tried to be slower. Walking less fast
I get there just as soon.
There's peace in slowness, and quietness
Like a summer afternoon:

Not as slow as a flower opening,
Nor as the waning moon,
Nor the silent passage of minutes
As morning moves towards noon,

But less like a raucous symphony
And more like a lilting tune,
Less like the chaos of January
And more like the kiss of June.

To a Rose, Given by a Friend

You came to me unexpectedly,
Deep velvety red, in bloom,
An elegant gift. I am honored
To have you here in my room.

What power and beauty was hidden
Inside you that led you to bloom,
Each petal so perfect, so fragrant:
A miracle, here in my room.

Exercise in Synonyms

Happy, joyful, cheerful, glad,
Crimson, blushing, rosy, red,
Irate, angry, fuming, mad,
Sleeping, dreaming, tucked in bed,
Tearful, moping, grieving, sad,
Sightless, soundless, heartless, dead.

Before the Dawn

Sky is dark and air is still,
    Quiet, hushed, serene,
No longer night but not yet day —
    A moment in between.

We hang in the eternal now,
    A silent mystery,
No past or future, good or bad:
    The always about-to-be.

Following

Spring will follow ice and snow,
    Sunshine follow rain,
Sleep will follow a busy day,
    And healing follow pain,
After hours of emptiness
    Ideas fill the brain.
So why does a heart that's broken
    Refuse to mend again?

Lesson from Comics

Biff! Bam! Pow!
They're down, they're out. And then,
In the next panel, good as new,
They're on their feet again.

Wouldn't it be nice
If we could do the same,
Bounce back as if we somehow knew
That life was just a game?

Holiday Gifts

Hanukkah candles and Christmas lights,
Presents for girls and for boys,
Eating together and singing together,
Games and confections and toys.
But more precious still are family and friends:
Our blessings, our comfort, our joys.

On Finishing a Good Book (II)

Dear book, I wish you were longer.
Why did you have to end?
Day by day, as I turned your pages,
You were a companion, a friend.

Chapter by chapter, we wandered
Through landscapes enchanting and new.
I loved you. I'll never forget you.
Will you remember me too?

To the New Moon

Dear moon, you are there in the evening sky,
    A thin, bright curve of delight,
With your arms embracing a pale, faint glow -
    The old moon, dim in the night.

Thank you, dear moon, for the memory,
    Sent down to me from above,
Of the years my own arms held children,
    Encircling them all with love.

Whatever

Whatever goes in comes out.
Whatever goes up comes down.
Whoever rides on the carousel
Likes to go round and round.

Whatever sleeps will wake.
Whatever begins will end.
Whoever cares for a dog or cat
Has found a loyal friend.

Whoever laughs and smiles,
Whoever drops some tears,
Will follow the same familiar path
As days move into years.

Whatever is born grows up.
Whatever grows up grows old.
Whoever lives and loves has riches
More precious than silver or gold.

Ode to the Letter J

Judy Garland,
Jane Eyre,
Jack & Jill and Jaws,
January blizzards,
January thaws,

Julia Child,
Joshua Tree,
Jungles, jaguars,
Junk, jalopies, jewelry,
Juices, jelly jars,

Jeremiah,
Josephine,
Job and Jackie O,
Judge & jury, justice,
Jonah down below,

John Doe,
Jacob's ladder,
Jazz and jamboree,
Jungle gyms and javelins,
Juno, jubilee,

Jane Austen,
Jesse James,
Jade in glossy greens,
Japanese beetles, jackals,
Jackets, jerkins, jeans,

Jenny Lind,
Jerusalem,
Jehovah, James the king,
Jabberwocky, jealousy,
Jasmine in the spring,

Juliette at her window,
Jupiter in the sky,
Jokes and jests
Jumping jacks,
June and then July,

Jack-in-the-pulpits,
Jackasses,
Juke box's jangly bellow,
Jackknife dives and jackpot wins,
Juicy Fruit gum and Jello,

Janis Joplin,
James Joyce,
Jokes for girls and boys,
Jaundice, jargon, juggernaut,
Jeopardy and joys,

Jack rabbits,
Jack-o'-lanterns,
Janitors, jails with locks,
Jackstraws and jackdaws,
Jay birds, Jack-in-the-Box,

Jimmy Durante,
James Dean,
Courageous Joan of Arc,
Jack Sprat who ate no fat,
Japheth in the ark,

Jimmy Stewart,
John of Gaunt,
John Jacob Astor too,
Jacks and jump ropes, journalism,
Jelly rolls to chew,

Jingle bells,
Jersey cows,
Jason on his quest,
Jams to spread on buttered bread —
But JELLYBEANS ARE BEST!

What is a Poem?

A poem is a feeling,
A poem is a thought,
A poem is a challenge, a song.
A poem can be angry, a hot diatribe,
An effort to right what's gone wrong.

A poem can silly,
A poem can be sad,
A love letter pleading, a dart,
But whatever it is and wherever it goes,
It always comes straight from the heart.

What's in a Name?

Ketchup & Mustard, Chocolate Sundaes,
Limeades and Liberties,
Rainbows and Rebels and Root Beer Floats,
Tigers and Bumblebees,
Snakes and Swirls and Starry Nights,
Cub Scouts and Christmas Trees,
Bricks and Bloodies and Benningtons,
Clambroths and Clearies — all these
Are only marbles, those rounds of glass,
To do with as we please!

Grown-up Children

How did those little babies
Become who they are today?
How does time work its wonders,
Silently, day after day?
We don't see it happen, or hear it,
We cannot speak. We are dumb:
The magic of what's behind us,
The mystery of what's to come.

Heavenly Harmony

Secrecy, sorcery, sympathy,
Privacy, parody, pie,
Anarchy, archery, alchemy,
Fallacy, family, fly,
Comedy, carpentry, calumny,
Revelry, rivalry, ray,
Ecstasy, energy, empathy,
Bakery, battery, bay,
Memory, mystery, monarchy,
Jewelry, jollity, joy,
Lunacy, leprosy, legacy,
Treachery, tragedy, toy!

Double Digits

Ten little fingers,
Ten little toes,
Tender feelings,
Tenement woes,
Tend the garden,
Water the rose,
Tents and tentacles,
Tenpins in rows,
Tenderloins, tenderfeet,
Friends or foes,
Tenors, tendencies,
So it goes,
Tennis matches —
But everyone knows
It all began with
Fingers and toes.

Old Friends (I)

Soft puppies, turtles,
Purring kittens, a rabbit:
You were my first loves.

Early Morning on the Roof

Stars fill the dark sky,
Dawn brings a glow to the hills,
Words float through my mind.

Three Pots with Paths and a Salamander

We travel our separate paths,
In sunny or stormy weather.
But parent or child or salamander,
We share this earth together.

Promise Me

I love you in the morning
     And I love you in the night,
I love you when the moon is up
     And when the sun is bright,
I want you there beside me
     Until our time is done.
I want two minds to share their dreams,
     Two hearts to beat as one.

Triplets

Girls and boys,
games and toys,
sorrows and joys.

Socks and shoes,
hints and clues,
greens and blues.

Kittens and pups
glasses and cups,
downs and ups.

Fingers and toes,
ribbons and bows,
highs and lows.

Pies and cakes,
rivers and lakes,
spiders and snakes.

Pennies and dimes,
lemons and limes,
rhythms and rhymes.

Lions and bears,
tables and chairs,
ladders and stairs.

Dogs and cats,
coats and hats,
balls and bats.

Sticks and stones,
gifts and loans,
muscles and bones.

Forks and spoons
mornings and noons,
Julys and Junes.

Days and nights,
quarrels and fights,
depths and heights.

Floods and droughts,
whispers and shouts,
ins and outs.

Birds and bees,
coffees and teas,
carrots and peas,
      elbows and knees,
      bushes and trees,
      ticks and fleas,
            skates and skis,
            crackers and cheese,
            ankles and knees,
                  thank you's and please,
                  oceans and seas,
                  you's and me's.

Ones, twos, threes!

Thoughts from a Memorial Service

Memories bind us together,
Sadness wraps us round,
We share our love and our stories,
Laughter and tears abound.

You are no longer with us,
But are you really so far?
You will live in our hearts forever:
You are part of who we are.

Reincarnation

Shall I come back as a flower,
        Dancing in wind and sun?
Or a quiet mossy wood,
        Bringing shade to everyone?

Or a puppy who keeps us laughing?
        Or a bird who sings from a tree?
Or a sandy beach or an ice cream cone?
        Whatever shall it be?

Pick something that makes us happy.
        What do we have to lose?
Won't it be nice when the time comes round?
        (Assuming that we can choose!)

Entreaty to One's Feet

Dear feet, you've carried me here and there,
Uphill and down and everywhere,
You've been my companions all these years,
Leading me safely through hopes and fears.
Don't fail me now, I need you still,
For now the going seems more uphill,
Don't ache, don't break, be steady, be clever.
We need each other now more than ever.

To the Full Moon

What are you telling us, there in the sky,
        you huge, mysterious golden eye?
Are you an omen for us below,
        a warning of something we need to know?
You're older than we are, I think you know
        more than we do here below.
What do you see with your icy eye
        as you silently move across the sky?

Counting-Out Jingle

Lemons & limes,
Nursery rhymes.
Trucks & cars,
Chocolate bars.
Bushes & trees.
Bumble bees.
Veggies & fruits,
Cowboy boots.
Tables & chairs,
Teddy bears.
Socks & shoes,
Kangaroos.
Aches & pains,
Railroad trains.
Rivers & streams,
Pleasant dreams!

We Wake Up Together: Song to the Far Hills

Dear hills, you guarded me through the night,
Silent and dark. With morning light
Caressing your brows, you stretch and yawn,
Bid dreams good-by and meet the dawn.

New Year's Song

New year,
New days,
New things to do,
New plans,
Resolutions,
Hooray for the new!

But don't discard
Everything old.
Remember, we are blessed
With old traditions
Old ways,
Things we've loved
For all our days:
Old clothes comfort us,
Old favorites please us . . .
And old friends are best!

To the Imported Vines that Started California's Vineyards

You came across the seas to us
Year after lovely year.
Like all our other immigrants,
You set your roots down here.
You gave us your beautiful bounty,
We came to love you well.
You were not meant to encounter
The burning fires of hell.
Dear vines, we wish your hidden roots
The blessings of sun and rain,
So you can rise from beneath the earth
　　　To bloom again.

Suiseki

A found stone,
Unmarked, alone.
You give us a landscape
Whose beauties increase.
You bring us a mystery,
You offer us peace.

Three Miracles

A mother's words to her sons

I may have sheltered you for a while
        before you decided to make an appearance in this world,
But I didn't make you.
You made yourselves.
From smiling, tumbling adventurers,
        you turned into strong, generous young men,
                able to love,
                able to survive challenges and suffering,
                able to make a difference in the world.

You are blankets of comfort
        in times of fear.
You are missiles of light
        in an often-dark world.
You are islands of stability
        in a tumultuous ocean of uncertainty.

You are miracles, each one of you.

Being Awake in the Middle of the Night

The world is sleeping around me now,
Silent and still and dark.
Animals dream their wandering dreams,
I am alone in the ark.

Comfort Foods

Milk and cookies,
        A Teddy Bear,
These are what we need.

A gentle hug,
        A purring kitten,
A warm blanket indeed,

Vanilla pudding,
        P.B. and J,
What else could anyone need?

Forget about money
        Or status or fame.
These are the things we need!

Hats

Straw hats, fedoras,
Shower caps for showers,
Sombreros, hard hats
For long working hours,

Sunbonnets, trilbies,
Baseball caps, berets,
Cowboy hats and pork pies,
Hoods for rainy days,

Busbys, bowlers, fezzes,
Football helmets, veils,
Knitted cloches, homburgs,
Top hats to go with tails,

Stocking caps and beanies,
Panama hats . . . but why
Can't we bare our heads so they'll be kissed
By wind and sun and sky?

In Praise of Napping

Babies nap in comfy cribs,
Birds nap in trees,
Cats and dogs nap everywhere,
Whenever they please.

We nap at certain times;
Usually we choose
The afternoon . . . but any hour
Befits that lovely snooze!

Leave Me Alone

Leaves from the trees fall slowly.
Leaves from a book turn fast.
Leave from the army is always too brief,
No matter how long it will last.
Enjoy your sabbatical leave,
It's a change of pace well-earned.
Leave me the grandfather's clock in your will.
Don't leave a stone unturned.
When my children leave home I miss them.
Ten minus seven leaves three.
Leave it right there! And leave me some room.
Give me leave to exist, to be me.

Life Plan

Winning and losing,
Sleeping and waking,
Planning and dreaming,
Giving and taking,

Asking and telling,
Coming and going,
Loving and hating,
Wondering, knowing,

Smiling and frowning,
Laughing and crying,
Hoping and fearing,
Living and dying.

Dare you!

Strawberry shortcake, apple pie,
Gelato, tiramisu,
Chocolate pudding, creme brûlée,
Toll House cookies too.
Butterscotch sundaes, birthday cake,
Cherry cobbler, eclairs,
Cheesecake, cream puffs, macaroons —
Give them up? Who dares???

Lines for the 4th of July

We won our independence years ago,
But do we truly act as if we're free?
Do we speak out against injustices?
Fight for those denied their liberty?
Protect the causes we believe are right?
We always need to be alert to find
The courage to defend the truest freedom:
The precious independence of the mind.

Hymn to Certain Appendages

Oh, lovely hands and lovely feet,
You've lasted all these years,
You've guided me through ups and downs,
Through happiness and tears.

What would I do without you,
Fo dancing, climbing stairs,
For turning pages, patting puppies,
Moving rocking chairs,

For waving, signing birthday cards,
For slicing cake or bread,
For wading in a backyard stream,
Or climbing into bed?

You may be sore or slowing down,
But stay by me, dear friends,
I need you with me every day,
Until our journey ends.

Parts of Speech

Adjectives are cheerful or they're sad,
Exuberant or beautiful or lame.
And adverbs tell us how, they move along
Ferociously or quickly or with shame.
But nouns! Now there's another cup of tea!
They anchor us, they're solid, they're for real.
And verbs! They urge us forward, wake us up,
They push us, make us laugh until we squeal.
So here's to you, companions of my heart —
Dear words, you feed my minutes, fill my days.
I struggle with you, play with you, and love
Your power to charm, to comfort, to amaze.

Patterns

West and east,
Famine and feast,
Suns and moons,
Midnights and noons,
Smiles and frowns,
Ups and downs,
Coming and going,
Wondering, knowing,
Sleeping and waking,
Searching and taking,
Loving and giving,
As long as we're living.

Nightly Mystery

Where did I go,
          last night in my dreams?
What did I do
          in the dark that seems
So strange to me now?
          Could it possibly be
That weird and dangerous
          person was me?

Waking

How can I wake from my midnight dream?
How can I leave behind
The fear and beauty of that strange world,
The realm of my sleeping mind?
Moving back to this earthly world
Of gravity, reason, and death
Is such a journey! How can it happen
Just between breath and breath?

What We Don't Understand

We know about evolution and genes,
We've studied the birds and the bees,
Science has taught us its rules and its laws
In all their complexities.
But for all our knowledge, there still remains
This magnificent mystery:
How can you be only you,
And how can I be me?

When I was a child, I spake as a child

I babbled and gurgled, I cried and I cooed,
I laughed (and made noises that surely were rude).
But is it so different now that I'm grown?
Some old behaviors remain, still my own.
Babbling and cooing have wandered away,
But laughter and tears are still with me today.

Advice

Don't run with scissors.
Don't play with your food.
Don't leave your bed unmade.
Don't make a mess.
And don't be late.
Don't leave that bill unpaid.

So many don'ts!
But here's the best:
Don't ever be afraid
To say "I love you."
Let those words
Begin the heart's parade.

Gifts from the Sky

Birds and bees and butterflies,
And wind and rain and snow,
Come from the air above us
As we wander to and fro,
Fall from the sky to deliver
Their blessings on us below.

Clothing

Socks & shoes,
Hats & coats,
Jeans & slacks & skirts,
Blouses, dresses,
Sweaters, sandals,
Turtlenecks & shirts,
Feather boas,
Cummerbunds,
Ascots, tutus, gowns,
Spats & tunics,
Cloaks & stoles,
Turbans, garlands, crowns,
Ruffles, feathers,
Diamonds, pearls,
Flounces, furbelows —
Do these make us more elegant
Or beautiful?
Who knows?

Counting-out Rhyme (II)

Up and down,
    go to town,
In and out,
    yell and shout,
Highs and lows,
    touch your toes,
Win and lose,
    socks and shoes,
Sticks and stones,
    ice cream cones,
Slow and fast,
    don't be last!

Doubling Up

Ginger ale and gingersnaps,
Gingerbread as well,
Everybody loves them,
As far as we can tell.

Raindrops and rainbows
And raincoats to wear.
Snowballs and snowplows
And snowflakes in the air.

Night lights and nightmares,
Nightshades - don't eat!
Ice cubes and icebergs,
Ice skates for our feet.

Foot bridges, footstools,
Footprints in the sand.
We undertake and underwrite
And sometimes understand.

Square meals and square root,
Square dance for fun.
Anywhere and anybody,
Surely anyone!

Handshakes and handouts
And handcuffs: beware!
Double deckers, double crosses —
Doubles everywhere!

Elegy for a Hummingbird (I)

A terrible surprise:
    you are here, on my terrace, so tiny, so elegant, so still,
    your little feet still clinging tightly to their perch,
    your colors still glistening,
    every feather perfect.

How could you die?
How could you leave us?

Can I soften my sadness over your loss
    with gratitude that you were with us for a time?

Beautiful bird,
    like us, your days on earth are numbered,
    your journey will come to an end when it must.
My wish for you is that it came quickly,
    without pain or fear.

We are blessed that you were with us for a while
    and gave us your energy and your beauty.

Meditation

"Quiet body, quiet mind." That's the start, to say
Those simple words. Now chatter calms and worries fade away,
Hands relax and frowns recede, and magically we may
Find again that place of peace, so many worlds away.
Our troubles, plans, decisions, all are left behind
As silently we settle down. And silently we find
We have no past or future, no time of any kind,
We're resting in the moment. Quiet body, quiet mind.

Everything is Minutes

Sometimes minutes pass slowly,
When you're lying awake in bed.
Sometimes they tumble and gallop along
And turn into hours instead.
And hours move on into days and nights
And weeks and months and years.
We fill the time as it moves along
With joy and laughter and tears.

Memories

Alphabet blocks,
Slippers and socks,
Puppies and kittens,
Knitted mittens,
Skips and hops,
Lollipops,
Owies and moans,
Ice cream cones,
Boots and hats,
Baseball bats,
Dolls and toys,
Girls and boys,
Rocking chairs,
Teddy bears,
Crayons and chalk,
Babytalk,
Jumping ropes,
Wishes and hopes,
Smiles and frowns,
Ups and downs,
Puddles and streams,
Desires and dreams.

Morning's Blessing

The morning's benediction arrives in different ways:
A cup of tea, a stretch, a yawn, the sun's first timid rays.
The past and future blend into a morning hymn of praise
For what's ahead and memories of mornings and of days.

Ode to a Snail

You've been put on this earth for a reason,
I believe you've a right to be here.
I handle you carefully, gently,
When I pick you up, year after year.
As I relocate you to the trash can,
I always ask for your pardon.
I wish you a snail's happy life span . . .
Just don't live it here in our garden!

One Way to Walk in the Rain

Wasn't it fun to step in puddles,
      Making that splashing sound?
Now we delicately step over
      Or carefully walk around.

If we have on good rubber boots
      (To keep us protected from rain)
We can recapture that innocent joy
      And do it all over again!

Another Way to Walk in the Rain

Splishy splashy through the puddles,
Hoodie drawn up high,
Drips and drops on nose and lashes,
'Neath a sodden sky.

All the world's a mystery,
Secret, silent, wet,
No past, no future, nothing
To remember or forget.

Water's Blessings

Cooling drinks that crank up from
    The bottom of the well,
Baths and showers, rainy days,
    Rivers, ocean's swell,
Streams and puddles, creeks and brooks . . .
    And even tears as well.

Old Friends (II)

Old Mother Hubbard and Robin Hood
And Mary Poppins too,
Humpty Dumpty and Flicka and Lad,
Mowgli and dear Baloo,
It seems that I knew you forever,
But when did our love affair start,
When you left the pages of all those books
And moved into my heart?

Happy New Year

Another year has ambled by
With pleasures and with pains,
With cloudy nights and starry skies,
With sunbeams and with rains.
So let us greet the coming year
With hopes, and let us say,
"Bring peace to us, and happiness,
And kindness every day."

On Being Where We Are

"Oh, to be young again!" Would I say that?
Would I go back to those days
When nothing was clear, and failure might come
In so many different ways?
We thought we were smart, we thought that we knew
So much, had the world at our feet;
That foolishness lasted forever, it seemed,
It was innocent, it was sweet.
But it was a dream, it wasn't for real.
I wouldn't go back there today.
The innocence and the uncertainty
Were risky. I'd trade them away
For some wrinkles and creases, some quieting down,
Some patience, acceptance, and rest.
When we learn how to live in the moment at hand
We find freedom at last. We are blessed.

Love

One foot in front of the other,
One lonely day at a time,
      But we're still a family,
      We're still together —
Love is the name of this rhyme!

Belief

Week by week and day by day,
We've moved along on our lonely way,
Missing the grasp of a hand in ours,
Hugs that warmed us and blessed the hours,
But we can believe that, fresh and new,
The world will return for me and you.

On Reading a Book for the Second (or Third) Time

Hello, old friend! It's me again,
Starting at Chapter One.
We'll be together as long as it takes
On this journey I've just begun.
I know your story, its ups and downs,
Its pleasures and treasures and pain.
I'll laugh with you, cry with you, struggle and hope,
As I move through your life again.
I know you so well, it comforts me
To be with you. So is it true
That as I caress you page by page,
You know me and love me too?

To Shakespeare

Think of all you have given us:
        lovers and rascals and kings,
Plots that compel and words that inspire,
        all those wonderful things.
You only hoped, as you wrote those words,
        they would bring an audience pleasure.
But what they brought to a waiting world
        was riches beyond measure.

Ode to Shoes

Slippers and sandals,
      Flip-flops and mocs,
Hiking boots worn with
      Our wooliest socks –
Shoes are for walking
      And keeping us warm,
Protecting our toes
      From the cold and the storm.
So, dear shoes, as we amble
      Our way down the street,
We thank you for tending
      Our two precious feet.

We Still Have Love

Arms cannot hold us, nor hands caress,
But love will see us through:
The bonds of friendship will still remain,
Beautiful, bold, and true.
I can survive with you as my friend,
And you . . . and you . . . and you.

Entreaty

Be near. Stay with me.
Hear me. Know my name.
If you are there, dear friend,
We have each other.
No matter how dark the sky,
No matter the threatening weather,
Even if distanced in the darkness,
We can survive together.

In Praise of Tears

Tears can fall for sadness,
Tears can fall for mirth,
Tears can fall for all the ways
We desecrate the earth.

When you leave the world, my love,
To meet the world above,
The salty drops that flow for you
Are tributes of my love.

Counting-Out Rhyme (III)

Glances,
glasses,
dark molasses.

Lemurs,
llamas,
silk pajamas.

Puppies,
kittens,
wooly mittens.

Clamor,
clutter,
peanut butter.

Roses,
rookies,
sugar cookies.

Bonds

Bonds can be ropes that tie us up,
Or duties that tie us down,
Bonds can be memories, lessons, or fears,
Threads that entangle through days and years,
Ties that reach up from below us
Or ties that reach down from above.
But the greatest ties are those that connect us,
The bonds of friendship and love.

To Our Friends (I)

Your faces were beauty,
Your voices were love.
Missing you aches like a pain.
But don't give up! Hang in there!
It's not forever —
We'll be together again.

In Times of Darkness

Where is hope?
Where is cheer?
Where has beauty gone?
Has endless night dropped down on us,
Without a hope of dawn?

Nothing's gone,
Only hidden
Under darkened air.
Hope is here,
And cheer is here,
And beauty's everywhere:
A baby laughs,
A flower blooms,
A hummingbird rides the air.

If we can look, then we can find
Beauty and hope and cheer.
Looking is loving,
Believing is finding.
What's hidden is truly here.

Thoughts while Sheltering in Place

Memories float to the surface these days
Of pleasures that we recall:
Walks and talks and restaurants,
Wandering the mall,
Ups and downs and ins and outs
Through summer, spring, and fall.
But it's hands that touch and arms that hold —
These are most precious of all.

To the Sun, about to appear over the hills

Come up, dear friend, and be with us,
We need the caress of your rays:
You're steady, dependable, powerful,
You sever the nights from the days,
You warm us, embrace us, and comfort us.
You'll watch over us always.

Door Questions

I am standing outside the door.
Will it open?
Can I go through it? . . . into what?
Will it close behind me?

> Where am I?
> Do I want to be here?
> Is it sunny here? or cloudy?
> Is it safe? or dangerous?
> Can I walk up the path ahead? or will I stumble and fall
> on broken stones?
> Who is waiting for me behind the trees?
> Will he enfold me in his arms and say, "You are beautiful.
> I love you."
> Or will he scowl and frown and lunge at me, a knife in
> his hand?
> Here's the big question: Can I go back though the door?

How can I choose?
Such possibilities!
Such openings before me!
So many roads to travel.
So many doors.

Ode to Ice Cream

Stuffed in a cone, precariously,
Cold and smooth and sweet,
There for our tongues to navigate —
You were always a treat.
We learned the way to catch the drips
From sliding down our wrist:
All it took was a waiting tongue
And an upward licking twist.
Years go by. You are still a treat,
To eat with a silver spoon,
Butter pecan with chocolate sauce,
Peppermint, macaroon.
But no matter the elegant setting,
The first bite will still begin
A backward trip through years of time
To a childhood still within.

Family Letter

Dear sisters and brothers,
Dear children and grands,
We cannot yet hug you,
We cannot hold hands,
But we are still bound
From below and above
With ties that connect
And enfold us with love.
We're not really separate,
We're not far apart,
We live side by side
In the realms of the heart.

Things that Come from the Sky

Birds and bees and butterflies,
Bats that flap their wings,
Rain and wind and snow and hail,
Through winters, summers, springs,
Sunshine, moonshine, starshine too,
And clouds that wander by,
The rainbow's magic curve - all these
Are blessings from the sky.

Yes, We Can: A Rallying Cry

We have lost the sense of oneness:
        one people, one nation, one heart.
When did it leave us? Where did it go?

Can we remember, all those dark years ago,
        when bombs rained down in Europe,
        our brothers in France and Italy and Brussels were dying,
        and children in London were afraid at night?
We were one then.
We were all different, but we came together
        as part of a whole that was greater than any of us,
        with shared hopes of peace and unity.

We need that again.
We need the wholeness.
To survive, we must be one.
We need to be one people, one nation, one heart.

We can find that belief in our oneness,
        it is within us still,
        it is waiting to emerge.
We can discover our unity again.
We can come together.

Let us be again a united whole.
Let us be the United States.

To Our Friends (II)

Your voices are music.
Your faces are love.
You bring us down warmth from the sun up above.

Your friendship enfolds us
And conquers our fears.
We need you beside us through days and through years.

Going Along

One foot in front of the other,
     One even breath at a time,
Sunrises, sunsets, mornings and noons,
     Words and rhythms and rhyme,
Sunshine and shadow, the path ahead,
     One steady step at a time.

Fourteen Haiku to Oakland

Dear Oakland, our home,
your energy keeps us warm
and blesses our hearts.

Your mix of people,
old and young, richer, poorer,
fills our hearts with love.

Bells ring out, dogs bark,
horns, whistles, children's laughter:
Oakland's sweet music.

Pelicans, grebes, coots,
herons, egrets, diving ducks
grace Lake Merritt's calm.

Cool cloudy mornings,
warmer sunny afternoons:
Oakland's soft springtime.

At night, Oakland's hills
become a dark tapestry
strung with tiny lights.

High buildings, low lake,
light and dark, noise and quiet:
Oakland's lovely mix.

Tent cities deface
our parks. But it's only luck
we aren't sleeping there.

Construction noise, shouts,
hammering, buildings rising:
Oakland's on the move.

Churches, synagogues,
chapels, mosques - voices rise to
the same Great Spirit.

Those who smash windows
come from the surrounding towns:
we march peacefully.

Old shoes, bottles, cans
false teeth, lie in Lake Merritt
with other good stuff.

We need our sports teams!
Our kids need to have heroes
to model their dreams.

Children laugh, dogs bark,
frisbees, sandwiches and juice:
picnics in the park.

Answer to the Poet

Dear Lorca —
New York is indeed a babble,
> a cacophony of light and sound and motion:
Neon lights,
> changing colors,
>> winking,
>>> blinking,
>>>> flashing,
Honking horns,
> voices hailing cabs,
>> talking,
>> quarreling,
>>> yelling,
People walking,
> shoving,
>> hurrying,
>>> hurrying,
>>>> hurrying . . .
Nothing is slow,
> nothing is quiet.
You've got it right.
But, dear Lorca,
I'm not so sure we can confuse the lights of the skyscrapers with stars.
> Stars are still,
>> far away,
>>> unchanging,
>>>> perfect.
Unlike New York, the stars anchor us, calm us, bring us peace.
One doesn't go to New York for peace,
> for other things perhaps,
>> but not for peace.

Homage to a Shoelace

You keep our shoes from falling off,
       A wise and useful thing to do!
You're dingy, wrinkled, tired, old,
       You look worn out along your length.
But you are precious, you are dear,
       You still have beauty, you have strength,
You don't complain, you do not break.
       We could do worse than be like you!

Listening to the Rain

Clouds will open,
Rain will fall,
To feed us, soothe us,
Bless us all.
Hear the message
From above:
Sounds of softness,
Sounds of love.

To a Poet

Hold fast to dreams,
*   for if dreams die,*
Life is a broken-winged bird that cannot fly.

Hold fast to dreams,
*   for when dreams go,*
Life is a barren field, frozen with snow.

Langston Hughes, you and I are different.

You are a man, I am a woman.
You are a renowned poet, I am just someone who
    likes putting words together.
You are black, I am white.
You grew up in a world of prejudice, I grew up in a world
    that felt safe and fair.
Your skin closed doors to you, my skin opened doors and
    opportunities.

We are so different. How can I know you?

And yet, we meet in your poetry.
I, too, hold on to dreams.
They buoy me up, they enrich my life, they give me
    a sense of the future.
Like you, I don't want to be a broken-winged bird
    or a barren field.

136

You hold out your poem to me, and I enter it.
In your poem our hands touch. We hold each other,
   for a moment.

It's only a moment
But that moment can last a lifetime.
Auden wrote, "Poetry makes nothing happen."
But maybe . . . maybe . . .
Maybe poetry can make something happen.
Maybe poetry can change the world.

On the Importance of Spelling

There's some and there's sum,
    Feet and feat,
Days and daze,
    Beat and beet,

There's great and grate,
    Blue and blew,
Peace and piece,
    Threw and through,

There's prince and prints,
    Horse and hoarse,
Heard and herd,
    Coarse and course,

There's hymn and him,
    Weight and wait,
Stair and stare,
    Eight and ate,

There's sense and cents,
    Plain and plane,
Birth and berth,
    Reign and rain,

There's won and one,
    Cruise and crews,
Made and maid,
    Choose and chews,

There's knew and new,
        Sleigh and slay,
There and their,
        Way and weigh,

There's waste and waist,
        Bare and bear,
Sight and site,
        Fare and fair,

There's here and hear,
        Sale and sail,
Sun and son,
        Pail and pale,

There's sweet and suite,
        Fleas and flees,
Knot and not,
        Seas and seize,

There's flower and flour
        Pour and pore,
Seen and scene,
        Sore and soar.

So we'd better be careful
        What letters we write -
We want to be sure
        We get it right!

To a Hockey Puck Used as a Paperweight

You are my best paperweight.
You are hard, black, solid rubber.
You are not too heavy; I can lift you and hold you in my hand.
But you have your own weight,
    you hold a stack of papers on my desk without slipping.

Without slipping . . . ?
In your own life, you did a lot of slipping.
Your form is perfect for what you needed to do,
    which was to slip around on the ice.

Do you have memories of your previous life held inside you?
    — how you whizzed along the frozen ice?
    — how it felt when you were whacked by a stick and
            sent careening to the far end of the rink?
    — or being passed back and forth as you led the way
            down the ice, the flashing skates following you,
            as you headed towards the goal?
    — and the cheer that rose all around you as you screamed
            into the net?
    — the noise and excitement of it all?
    — the violence of the game?

And how about my memories?

> I watched my sons playing hockey,
>> happy teenagers engaged in a sport they worked hard at
>> and so enjoyed.
> I cheered them on as they moved, and you moved,
>> round and round on the ice.

Are my memories also alive in you?

As you sit here on my desk,

> anchoring my papers,

> far from the frozen world you knew so well,

Does my love for the boys who moved so smoothly with you

> on the frozen ice
> continue to live in you,
> as it lives in me and continues to warm my heart?

Hymn to Flowers

Peonies, poppies, and pansies,
Daisies and dahlias too,
Larkspur and lilies and lilacs,
And gentians' sweet secretive blue,
Crocuses, clover, carnations,
Hollyhocks standing so tall,
Anemones and alyssum,
And asters that welcome the fall,
Hyacinths and hydrangeas,
Honeysuckle so sweet,
Buttercups and begonias,
Foxglove (but do not eat!),
And don't forget tulips and roses,
And orchids and zinnias too —
Sweet blossoms, you bless our dear planet,
And we send our love back to you.

Messages

Messages can be written on paper
Or typed on computer keys
Or spoken or shouted or sent by mail
To be received with ease.
But wordless messages also float
Up to the realms above
To those who have gone before us,
Borne on the wings of love.

Pairs (II)

Wrists and ankles,
      elbows and knees,
Lunches and suppers,
      thank you and please,
Mornings and evenings,
      laughter and tears,
Floating along through
      our days and our years.

Back and Forth

Hard & easy,
Happy, sad,
Loving, hating,
Good & bad,

Short & tall,
Above, below,
Searching, finding,
Come & go,

Sunny, shady,
Up & down,
Sad & happy.
Smile, frown,

Neat & messy,
In & out,
Winning, losing,
Whisper, shout,

Beginning, ending,
Waking, sleeping,
Full & empty,
Laughing, weeping,

Forget, remember,
Young & old,
Few & many,
Timid, bold,

Forgiving, blaming,
High & low,
Alone, together,
To & fro,

Giving, taking,
Loose & tight,
Noisy, quiet,
Day & night,

Winter, summer,
Wet & dry,
Wide & narrow,
Live & die,

Same & different,
Work & play,
Weave a pattern
Day by day.

How to Enjoy the Day

Cakes and pies,
Open your eyes,
Bacon and eggs,
Stretch your legs,
Peaches and plums,
Twiddle your thumbs,
Chips and fish,
Make a wish,
P b and j,
Laugh and play,
Lemons and limes,
Counting-out rhymes,
A roll and a bun,
Have lots of fun,
Apples and pears,
Climb the stairs,
Jam and bread,
Jump into bed.

Walking Song
Tribute to the Seven Dwarfs

Hi-ho, hi-ho,
Please join us as we go
Along our way
From day to day,
Through sun and rain and snow.
We struggle on
From evening up to dawn,
Through hopes and fears,
Through days and years.
Hi-ho! But this is what we know:
We need each other,
Sister, brother,
Singing as we go.
Whatever the weather,
We'll make it together,
So come along. Hi-ho!

Who Makes the Best Pet?

Gerbils are tiny and soft in your hand,
      In their wheel they go round and round.
Rabbits move with a hippity-hop
      And never make a sound.
Parrots' feathers are gorgeous and gay
      But they flap their wings and squawk.
Ponies will nuzzle you gently and soft
      Or take you around for a walk.
Kittens are cute, and grown-up cats
      Will lie in your lap and purr.
Goldfish will wave their fins at you
      If you give their tanks a stir.
Turtles lie still and sun themselves
      And snap at fleas and flies.
But dogs will lean against your side
      With love-light in their eyes.

Try a Jigsaw Puzzle

As I lovingly handle each tile,
Fitting carefully one with another,
So the fragments blend into a picture
That is whole, and foretells sunny weather,
Is each piece a piece of myself?
As I nestle them one with another,
Is it me I am really creating?
Am I putting myself back together?

Sing A Song

Sing a song of happiness:
  Spring is almost here!
Winter spills and winter chills
  Will fade and disappear.
Buds will open, birds will sing,
  Warm skies will soon appear.
Sing a song of happiness:
  Laughter, hope, and cheer.

What Are Good Dreams Made Of ?

Not fame, and not money
Or the power it brings —
What we need in our sleep
Are much simpler things:
Twenty-four colors
In a crayon box,
A new library book,
A clean pair of socks,
Tumbling puppies
And cuddly kittens,
A comfy old sweater
And warm woolen mittens,
Hot buttered toast
And vanilla ice cream:
These are the blessings
We want in a dream.

Homage to the AIDS Quilt

Your cloth oblongs reach out to me,
Your bright threads call to me,
They touch my heart
       and awaken grief for all of you who have left us.
Your words so carefully stitched,
       weaving up and down and across
       in glowing rainbow colors,
       some misspelled,
       some beautifully surrounding pictures,
Summon a well of despair
       for all those of you who lie in those fabric graves.
But living with you here on our wall,
       seeing you every time I walk by you,
       having you close enough to touch,
Distills the grief,
       and enlarges the despair into a swell of love:
Love for all of you who are gone,
       our sons and brothers
       and those we never knew,
And love for those of you who are still here.
And the love merges with gratitude
       for those of you we had with us for a while
       and those of you we still have,
       living and breathing beside us.

Survival Song

As soon as we felt our mother's arms
Enfold us and hold us, we knew
That to live and survive we need each other;
Whatever the time and whatever the weather,
We need the touch of a loving hand,
A heart that listens and understands.
We know this is true: we have each other.
We are not alone. We survive together.

Thoughts for a Memorial Service

Memories bind us together,
Sadness wraps us round,
We share our love and our stories,
Laughter and tears abound.
You are no longer with us,
But are you really so far?
You will live in our hearts forever,
Because of who you are.

Elegy for a Hummingbird (II)

Dear lovely little bird, you honored us:
You choose our roof to build your tiny nest.
You warmed your precious eggs. You lived and breathed
Through rain and wind and sleet. You did your best.
Now you are gone. We hope your end was quick.
We miss you now. Your memory is blessed.

Good-by, Dear Friend

Dear friend, without you here,
The world is an emptier place.
I miss your loving energy,
I miss your beautiful face.
How many days did I have you?
How many weeks and years?
How many cups of coffee?
How many smiles and tears?
How many rainy evenings?
How many sunny days?
They're countless. And now I miss you
In numberless, countless ways.

Good-by, Beloved

In sadness we lay you to rest,
Wrapped in our love for a cover,
With aching hearts we give you
Back to the earth, your mother.

To Our Bodies

We've lived in our bodies for years and years,
They've danced us through laughter and held us through tears.
So dear arms and dear legs, dear fingers and toes,
Dear lungs, brains, and kidneys, dear eyes, ears, and nose,
I love you and thank you for all that you do,
And believe in my heart that you cherish me too.

To a Cane

Dear Cane, you're here beside me now,
We wander forward, to and fro.
I trust your balance. Step by step
We move together, fast or slow.
You are a friend who holds my hand
And walks with me, where e'er I go

In the Beginning was the Word

Just think of the poems we have heard,
From heartfelt to light and absurd,
      Their power is old,
      Their force is untold —
At the start of all Time was the Word.

Notes

Mt. Tamalpais
Mount Tamalpais is the highest peak in the Marin Hills north of San Francisco.

Lake Merritt, Seen from Above
Lake Merritt is located within the city of Oakland.

One Nation, Indivisible: A Meditation on Proposition 8
In 2008, Proposition 8 defined marriage in California as between one man and one woman. A Court struck down the amendment in 2010, ruling it violated the U.S. Constitution.

To the Clay Room
In St. Paul's Towers, where sculpture classes were held. Also see *On Making a Clay Relief of a Stone Carving*, p. 39

Syllable Syllabub
Syllabub is a frothy or creamy dessert, often made with alcohol, first popularized in Britain in the 16th century.

Ode to Matisse's Etruscan Vase
Interior with an Etruscan Vase (1940), by Henri Matisse

Lentando
Lentando: with a gradual decrease in speed.

Suiseki
6th c. Japanese art involving the collection, display, and appreciation of a stone, without altering its shape or appearance, often to evoke mountains, waterfalls, or other scenes in nature.

Answer to the Poet
Poet in New York (1929) by Frederico Garcia Lorca.

To a Poet
> "Hold fast to dreams," from "Dreams" (1923) by Langston Hughes

Homage to the AIDS Quilt
> Each panel of the quilt is a personalized memorial for someone lost to HIV/AIDS. As of 2024 there are roughly 50,000 panels for more than 110,000 individuals.

Some Poetic Forms Used

Triolet
> A fixed verse form of eight lines with two rhymes, originating in thirteenth-century France. The final word of line one is repeated at the end of lines four and seven, while the second line is repeated in the final line.

Sonnet
> Fourteen lines in iambic pentameter (ten syllables alternating between unstressed and stressed). The form originating in thirteenth-century Italy uses an eight-line stanza followed by a six-line stanza, in a variety of rhyme schemes.

Haiku
> Three unrhymed lines of five, seven, and five syllables. While its roots are ancient, this familiar form emerged in seventeenth-century Japan. Haiku traditionally deal with seasons and the world of nature.

Pantoum
> A fifteenth-century Malaysian form of four-line stanzas in which the second and fourth lines of each stanza serve as the first and third lines of the next stanza. A pantoum can be of any length, and its final line often echoes its first.

Index of Titles